DISCOVERING THE NETHERLANDS

A COMPREHENSIVE TRAVEL GUIDE

BY

WILLIAM JONES

2023

Contents

Preface

In the intricate web of Europe's cultural mosaic, the Netherlands stands as a gem—a nation that beckons with its rich history, artistic legacy, innovative spirit, and a landscape adorned with tulip fields and iconic windmills. As we commemorate the first anniversary of "Discovering the Netherlands: A Comprehensive Travel Guide," it is with great pleasure and a sense of nostalgia that I reflect on the journey we embarked upon a year ago.

In the realm of travel, the Netherlands occupies a distinctive place. It is a country where medieval charm seamlessly coexists with cutting-edge modernity, where tulips bloom in vibrant hues against a backdrop of historic canals, and where the spirit of exploration and trade has left an indelible mark on the very fabric of its cities. This guide is not merely a compendium of facts and itineraries; rather, it is an invitation to embark on a voyage of discovery, to traverse the cobbled streets of ancient towns, to meander along canals that whisper tales of centuries past, and to partake in the cultural tapestry woven by the Dutch people.

The journey begins in Amsterdam, the cosmopolitan capital that proudly wears its cultural heart on its sleeve. As you navigate the city's maze of canals and cycle-friendly streets, you'll encounter the masterpieces of the Dutch Golden Age in world-renowned museums, witness the juxtaposition of historic architecture and contemporary design, and immerse yourself in the vibrant energy of a city that thrives on diversity and creativity.

Moving southward, Rotterdam unveils itself as a testament to resilience and rebirth. Once ravaged by war, this city has risen from the ashes to become a showcase of modern architecture and urban innovation. Rotterdam's skyline, adorned with daring structures like the Erasmus Bridge and the Cube Houses, reflects a forward-thinking spirit that complements the country's rich historical legacy.

The Hague, the political nucleus of the Netherlands, invites exploration of its regal past. Amidst grand palaces and governmental edifices, you'll discover the Binnenhof, the historical heart of Dutch politics, and the Mauritshuis Museum, home to Vermeer's iconic "Girl with a Pearl Earring." The Hague's stately elegance offers a captivating contrast to the lively ambiance found in Amsterdam.

Utrecht, with its medieval charm and the imposing presence of the Dom Tower, beckons travelers to unravel its history. As you traverse the city's narrow streets, adorned with wharf cellars and historic façades, a sense of timelessness pervades, transporting you to an era where trade and culture flourished along the banks of the Rhine.

The journey then leads to Giethoorn, the enchanting "Venice of the North," where car-free canals wind their way through thatched-roof houses and lush greenery. In this idyllic setting, time seems to slow down, offering a peaceful respite from the hustle and bustle of modern life.

Haarlem, a stone's throw from Amsterdam, invites exploration of its artistic heritage. The Frans Hals Museum, dedicated to the works of the Dutch Golden Age, stands as a testament to Haarlem's contribution to the world of art. The Grote Markt, surrounded by historic buildings, provides a picturesque backdrop for leisurely strolls and cultural immersion.

Delft, renowned for its iconic blue-and-white pottery, captivates with its charming streets and historic landmarks. The Royal Delft Factory opens a window into the intricate process of creating the famed Delftware, while the Markt square offers a delightful blend of artisanal shops and inviting cafes.

Maastricht, nestled in the southernmost reaches of the Netherlands, tantalizes the senses with its culinary delights. The Vrijthof square, surrounded by medieval architecture, becomes a stage for cultural events, and the Maas River offers a scenic backdrop to leisurely walks and gourmet experiences.

Venturing into the natural realm, the guide explores the Netherlands' national parks, where diverse landscapes unfold. From the Hoge Veluwe's heathlands and forests to the wetlands of De Biesbosch and the coastal ecosystems of Oosterschelde, each park reveals a unique facet of the country's natural beauty.

As spring blankets the Dutch landscape, the chapter on Tulip Season guides you through a spectacle of color. From the meticulously manicured gardens of Keukenhof to the vast fields of blooming tulips, this season paints the Netherlands in hues that evoke wonder and awe.

This guide is not a static document but a living testament to the dynamic nature of travel. The Netherlands, with its ever-evolving cities, landscapes, and cultural offerings, continues to inspire exploration. As you embark on your journey through these pages, may you find not just information, but an invitation to engage with the soul of the Netherlands—a country that seamlessly bridges the past and the present, tradition and innovation.

Happy travels,

William Jones Author, "Discovering the Netherlands: A Comprehensive Travel Guide"

Introduction

In the intricate tapestry of European nations, the Netherlands emerges as a captivating thread, weaving together a narrative of history, innovation, natural splendor, and cultural richness. As you stand at the threshold of this travel guide, contemplating the journey that lies ahead, allow me to be your guide, your companion in unraveling the stories that have shaped this small yet significant country.

The Netherlands, often colloquially referred to as Holland, beckons with a unique allure that transcends its modest geographical size. Nestled in the northwestern corner of Europe, bordered by Germany to the east, Belgium to the south, and the North Sea to the northwest, the Netherlands is a land of contrasts and harmonies. From the medieval charm of its historic towns to the cutting-edge architecture of its modern cities, from the serene landscapes of its national parks to the vibrant palette of tulip fields in spring, this is a nation that offers a kaleidoscope of experiences.

This travel guide is a key to unlock the treasures of the Netherlands. It is an exploration not just of physical landscapes but of the historical imprints, cultural nuances, and the ever-evolving identity of a nation shaped by water, wind, and an indomitable spirit of exploration.

A Historical Tapestry

To understand the essence of the Netherlands, one must trace the contours of its history, a narrative etched with tales of resilience, innovation, and a symbiotic relationship with the forces of nature. The Dutch Golden Age, spanning the 17th century, is a pivotal chapter in this story. It was a time when Dutch art, science, and trade flourished, and the Republic of the Seven United Netherlands emerged as a global maritime power.

The legacy of this era is palpable in the architecture of Amsterdam's canal-side houses, the masterpieces displayed in the Rijksmuseum, and the intricate merchant houses of historic towns. As you navigate the narrow streets of Utrecht, where the silhouette of the Dom Tower stands as a sentinel to centuries past, or wander through the halls of the Mauritshuis in The Hague, home to Vermeer's iconic works, you are traversing the corridors of time.

The historical narrative is not confined to grand palaces and museums alone. It resonates through the cobbled streets of Delft, where the echoes of Johannes Vermeer's life linger, and in the medieval squares of Haarlem, where the spirit of the Dutch Golden Age is palpable. Each city and town bears witness to the ebb and flow of historical currents, leaving an indelible mark on the cultural landscape.

Cultural Resonance

Beyond its historical narrative, the Netherlands is a canvas adorned with the brushstrokes of cultural richness. Amsterdam, often hailed as the "Venice of the North," is not merely a city of canals and coffee shops but a cultural hub that pulsates with artistic energy. The Van Gogh Museum immerses visitors in the tumultuous brilliance of the artist's mind, while the Anne Frank House serves as a poignant reminder of the human spirit's endurance in the face of adversity.

Rotterdam, a city reborn from the ashes of World War II, embraces modernity with a fervor reflected in its avant-garde architecture. The Cube Houses, designed by Piet Blom, defy conventional norms, symbolizing Rotterdam's commitment to innovation and creativity. Meanwhile, The Hague, the political epicenter, exudes a regal charm, inviting exploration of the Binnenhof and the elegant Mauritshuis.

In the southern city of Maastricht, culinary delights become a cultural expression. The Vrijthof square, surrounded by medieval architecture, transforms into a stage for cultural events, while the Maas River sets the scene for leisurely strolls along its picturesque banks. The diverse cultural landscapes of the Netherlands reveal themselves not only in museums and theaters but also in the everyday life of its cities and towns.

Nature's Symphony

While the urban landscapes tell stories of human endeavor, the Netherlands' natural beauty is a testament to harmonious coexistence. The national parks, scattered across the country, invite exploration into ecosystems that range from expansive heathlands to serene wetlands. Hoge Veluwe National Park, with its diverse landscapes and the Kröller-Müller Museum, offers a unique blend of nature and art.

De Biesbosch, one of Europe's last remaining freshwater tidal areas, provides a sanctuary for diverse flora and fauna. As you navigate its waterways, you enter a realm where nature's rhythm sets the pace. Oosterschelde National Park, with its tidal flats and dynamic marine life, stands as a living testament to the Netherlands' commitment to environmental conservation.

Tulips and Beyond

No exploration of the Netherlands is complete without the iconic tulip fields that carpet the landscape in spring. The chapter on Tulip Season is not merely a guide to vibrant blooms but an immersion into a tradition that dates back to the 17th century. Keukenhof Gardens, often hailed as the "Garden of Europe," becomes a canvas where tulips, daffodils, and hyacinths paint a landscape of unparalleled beauty.

Beyond the kaleidoscope of tulips, the Netherlands offers a mosaic of experiences. Giethoorn, with its car-free canals and thatched-roof houses, invites you to step into a fairy-tale setting. Haarlem, with its medieval architecture and artistic heritage, unveils a city that has inspired painters and poets alike. These experiences, diverse yet interconnected, form the essence of Dutch travel.

Embarking on the Journey

As you embark on this journey through the pages of "Discovering the Netherlands," envision yourself cycling along Amsterdam's canals, standing atop the Dom Tower in Utrecht, or indulging in a culinary feast along the Maas River. This guide is not a prescriptive manual but an invitation to engage with the soul of a nation that encapsulates the spirit of exploration, cultural richness, and natural beauty.

Prepare to traverse a landscape where windmills stand as sentinels, tulips sway in the breeze, and canals weave tales of trade and tradition. Whether you are a first-time visitor or a seasoned traveler seeking deeper insights, the Netherlands awaits with open arms.

So, as the pages turn, let the journey begin.

Amsterdam - The Cultural Heart

In the annals of European cities, few can rival the eclectic charm and cultural magnetism of Amsterdam. As the capital and largest city of the Netherlands, Amsterdam stands not only as a geographic center but also as a pulsating cultural heart that beats to the rhythm of history, art, and innovation. It is a city where the meandering canals, historic architecture, and world-class museums coalesce to create an immersive tapestry of experiences for the discerning traveler.

Historical Resonance

To understand the essence of Amsterdam, one must first navigate its historical contours. The city's origin can be traced back to the 12th century when a dam was constructed on the Amstel River, giving birth to "Amstelredamme" or Amsterdam. What began as a modest fishing village burgeoned into a trading powerhouse during the Dutch Golden Age of the 17th century.

The echoes of this Golden Age are palpable as one meanders through the city's UNESCO-listed canal ring. The Canal Ring, a network of concentric waterways lined with elegant townhouses, reflects a city that burgeoned during an era when commerce, art, and intellectual pursuits flourished. The canal system, an engineering marvel of the time, not only facilitated trade but also bestowed upon Amsterdam its distinctive character. As you stroll along these waterways, cross iconic bridges, and witness the dance of light on the canal surfaces, you are immersed in a living testament to Amsterdam's historical significance.

Museums and Masterpieces

Amsterdam's cultural canvas is perhaps most vividly painted within the hallowed walls of its museums. The Rijksmuseum, a repository of Dutch art and history, stands as a crown jewel. Home to masterpieces by Rembrandt, Vermeer, and other luminaries of the Dutch Golden Age, the Rijksmuseum is a journey through time, offering insights into the artistic and historical legacy that defines the Netherlands.

Adjacent to the Rijksmuseum, the Van Gogh Museum pays homage to the tormented genius whose post-impressionist works have left an indelible mark on the art world. The museum not only showcases Van Gogh's iconic paintings but also provides a glimpse into the artist's tumultuous life through letters and personal artifacts. A visit to this cultural haven is a profound encounter with the mind of a visionary.

The Anne Frank House, nestled along the Prinsengracht canal, is a poignant reminder of the human spirit's resilience in the face of adversity. The secret annex, where Anne Frank and her family hid from the Nazis during World War II, has been preserved as a museum. Walking through the concealed rooms and reading Anne's diary entries, visitors are transported to a time of persecution and courage, leaving an indelible imprint on their collective memory.

Canals and Architecture

The canals of Amsterdam, often referred to as the "Venice of the North," are not merely picturesque waterways but arteries that course through the city's cultural and historical veins. The Canal Ring, a UNESCO World Heritage site, is a testament to urban planning ingenuity. Lined with gabled houses that bear witness to centuries past, the canals create an ever-evolving cityscape that marries the old with the new.

Each canal possesses a distinct character. The Herengracht, known as the "Gentlemen's Canal," is adorned with stately merchant houses, while the Keizersgracht exudes a regal ambiance with its grand residences and tree-lined promenades. The Prinsengracht, hosting the Anne Frank House, is a tapestry of history and reflection. Cruising along these canals, whether by boat or on foot, unveils Amsterdam's architectural diversity, from the medieval structures of the Old Church to the modernist designs of the NEMO Science Museum.

The iconic canal houses, characterized by narrow facades and tall, slender profiles, are architectural marvels that reflect the city's past and present. These houses, many of which date back to the 17th century, were built on wooden piles driven into the marshy ground, a feat of engineering that attests to Amsterdam's resilience against the encroaching waters.

Culinary Explorations

Amsterdam's cultural allure extends beyond its artistic and historical treasures to the realm of gastronomy. The city's culinary landscape is a fusion of traditional Dutch fare and international influences, reflecting its role as a global hub of trade and commerce.

The Jordaan district, once a working-class neighborhood, has evolved into a culinary hotspot, offering a medley of trendy cafes, artisanal bakeries, and Michelin-starred restaurants. The Foodhallen, located in a converted tram depot, is a gastronomic paradise where visitors can savor a diverse array of international cuisines under one roof.

Traditional Dutch treats, such as stroopwafels (thin waffle cookies filled with caramel syrup) and poffertjes (small, fluffy pancakes), beckon from street vendors and local markets. Meanwhile, the vibrant De Pijp district is a melting pot of flavors, featuring a kaleidoscope of ethnic eateries serving everything from Surinamese roti to Middle Eastern falafel.

Vibrant Neighborhoods

Beyond the historic city center, Amsterdam's neighborhoods add layers to its cultural tapestry. De Wallen, known as the Red Light District, is not merely a hub of nightlife but also an area with a rich history. The Oude Kerk, Amsterdam's oldest surviving building, stands as a silent witness to the district's transformation over the centuries.

The Jordaan, with its narrow streets and quirky boutiques, exudes a bohemian atmosphere. This district, once home to working-class residents, has become a haven for artists, musicians, and those seeking an authentic Amsterdam experience. The Westergasfabriek, a former gasworks turned cultural complex, epitomizes the neighborhood's artistic and creative spirit.

The De Pijp district, south of the city center, offers a multicultural experience with its diverse population and eclectic mix of shops, cafes, and markets. The Albert Cuyp Market, a bustling street market, is a microcosm of Amsterdam's vibrancy, where locals and visitors alike converge to sample international cuisines, shop for eclectic wares, and soak in the dynamic atmosphere.

Cycling Culture

No exploration of Amsterdam is complete without delving into its quintessential mode of transportation—the bicycle. Amsterdam's cycling culture is not just a practical means of getting around but an integral part of its identity. With an extensive network of bike paths, dedicated lanes, and bike-friendly urban planning, Amsterdam is a city designed for two wheels.

Cycling along the canals, through the Vondelpark, or across the historic bridges offers a unique perspective of the city's charm. Bicycles are not mere conveyances; they are a cultural symbol, embodying the city's commitment to sustainability, health, and a leisurely pace of life.

Conclusion

As the sun sets over the gabled rooftops and the lights of Amsterdam begin to shimmer in the canals, one cannot help but feel a sense of having traversed not just through physical spaces but through epochs of history, corridors of artistic brilliance, and the vibrant tapestry of a city that breathes culture.

Amsterdam, with its storied past and dynamic present, remains a cultural heart that continues to beat in harmony with the ebb and flow of time. Whether one is drawn to the masterpieces of the Rijksmuseum, the reflections on the tranquil canals, or the eclectic flavors of its culinary scene, Amsterdam beckons as a city where every street corner, every bridge, and every museum holds a story waiting to be discovered.

As you navigate the streets and canals, allow Amsterdam to unravel its secrets, invite you into its embrace, and leave an indelible mark on your cultural wanderings. For in the cultural heart of Amsterdam, the journey is not just a physical exploration but a profound encounter with a city that has woven its history, art, and spirit into the very fabric of its being.

And so, as the dawn of a new day heralds fresh explorations, let Amsterdam be both your guide and your muse, inviting you to delve deeper into its cultural heart, where every moment becomes a brushstroke in the masterpiece of your own Amsterdam experience.

Rotterdam - Modern Marvels

In the southwestern reaches of the Netherlands, where the Maas River winds its way toward the North Sea, a city rises from the vestiges of wartime destruction with a fervor that embodies resilience and innovation. Rotterdam, often hailed as the "Gateway to Europe," is a city that wears its modernity proudly, juxtaposing sleek, avant-garde architecture against the remnants of a past marked by devastation. As one traverses the urban landscape of Rotterdam, a city reborn from the ashes of World War II, it becomes apparent that this metropolis is not merely a collection of buildings but a testament to human determination, creative expression, and the relentless pursuit of progress.

Resilience Rising from Ruins

The story of Rotterdam's transformation is inseparable from the ravages of war. In May 1940, during the early days of World War II, German bombing raids laid waste to much of the city, reducing its historic center to rubble. The post-war reconstruction, guided by a vision that embraced modernism and functionality, set the stage for the Rotterdam that exists today.

The city's commitment to rebuilding was not merely an exercise in restoring physical structures but a deliberate choice to redefine its identity. Unlike other European cities that opted for historical preservation, Rotterdam chose a path of bold, innovative reconstruction. The result is a cityscape that stands as a testament to the transformative power of architectural daring.

Iconic Architecture Defying Convention

Rotterdam's skyline is a symphony of modernist masterpieces, each structure vying for attention with its audacious design and avant-garde aesthetics. At the forefront of this architectural renaissance stands the Erasmus Bridge, an iconic cable-stayed bridge that spans the Maas River. Designed by Ben van Berkel, this graceful structure, often likened to a swan, has become the symbol of Rotterdam's modernity, connecting the north and south banks of the river with elegance and engineering prowess.

Adjacent to the Erasmus Bridge, the Kop van Zuid district beckons with a skyline punctuated by the vertical thrust of De Rotterdam. Designed by Rem Koolhaas, this colossal building complex, comprised of three interconnected towers, is a testament to Rotterdam's ambition. Its verticality not only defies traditional architectural norms but also reflects the city's determination to rise above its wartime scars.

The Cube Houses, or Kubuswoningen, designed by Piet Blom, are another architectural marvel that graces Rotterdam's urban landscape. A cluster of tilted, cube-shaped residences seemingly suspended in the air, the Cube Houses challenge the conventional notion of living spaces. As visitors traverse the pedestrian bridge that winds through these tilted cubes, they become part of an artistic exploration of space and perception.

Markthal, a horseshoe-shaped residential and office building, doubles as a vibrant food market with a ceiling adorned by a massive mural of fresh produce. The combination of residential and commercial spaces within a single structure is a reflection of Rotterdam's commitment to integrated urban planning. Designed by MVRDV architects, Markthal is not just a marketplace but an immersive experience where architecture, food, and culture converge.

The Modern City Center

Rotterdam's modernity extends beyond individual architectural landmarks to encompass the entire city center. The Lijnbaan, Europe's first pedestrianized shopping street, is a reflection of post-war urban planning principles. Flanked by modernist buildings and lined with shops and cafes, the Lijnbaan is both a commercial hub and a public space where residents and visitors alike can engage in leisurely strolls.

The Laurenskwartier, Rotterdam's historic heart, presents a harmonious blend of old and new. The Laurenskerk, a Gothic church that miraculously survived the wartime bombings, stands as a silent witness

to the city's resilience. Adjacent to the church, the modernist Timmer-
huis, designed by OMA architects, seamlessly integrates with its historical surroundings. This architectural juxtaposition symbolizes Rotterdam's commitment to preserving its heritage while embracing the future.

Cultural Enclaves and Waterfront Wonders

Rotterdam's modern marvels are not confined to its skyline alone;
they extend to cultural institutions that enrich the city's fabric. The Kun-
sthal, a contemporary art museum designed by Rem Koolhaas, is a dynamic space that hosts a diverse array of exhibitions. Its rotating displays
of visual arts, design, and photography contribute to Rotterdam's cultural vibrancy.

The Maritime Museum, situated in the historic Leuvehaven harbor,
is a celebration of Rotterdam's maritime legacy. The museum showcases
the city's historical connection to the sea, from its role as a trading port in
the Golden Age to its modern-day prominence as one of Europe's largest
ports. Visitors can explore historic vessels, maritime artifacts, and immersive exhibitions that delve into Rotterdam's seafaring past.

Winding along the Maas River, the Wilhelminapier is a waterfront
district that encapsulates Rotterdam's modernity and cosmopolitan atmosphere. The New Luxor Theater, with its contemporary design and
theatrical productions, is a cultural beacon, while the De Rotterdam
building complex adds a touch of architectural grandeur to the waterfront.

Sustainable Initiatives

Rotterdam's commitment to modernity extends to sustainability and
urban innovation. The city, cognizant of environmental challenges, has
embraced initiatives to create a greener, more resilient urban environment. The Dakpark, an elevated park on the roof of a shopping mall, is a
testament to Rotterdam's creative approach to maximizing green spaces
in the midst of urban development.

The Sustainable Building, a consortium of three interconnected
buildings, showcases cutting-edge sustainable practices in architecture.

From green roofs to energy-efficient technologies, this structure exemplifies Rotterdam's dedication to environmentally conscious urban planning. The city's commitment to sustainability aligns with its overarching vision of a future where modernity and eco-consciousness coalesce.

Culinary Renaissance

Rotterdam's modernity is not confined to its architectural and urban landscapes; it extends to its gastronomic scene. The city's diverse population, influenced by its status as an international trading hub, has fostered a culinary renaissance. From innovative Michelin-starred restaurants to multicultural street food markets, Rotterdam's dining scene is a reflection of its cosmopolitan spirit.

Witte de Withstraat, a vibrant street in the city center, is a culinary hub with an array of restaurants, cafes, and bars. Here, international cuisines and avant-garde dining experiences coexist, creating a gastronomic tapestry that mirrors Rotterdam's diversity. Food enthusiasts can savor everything from traditional Dutch dishes to contemporary culinary creations, all within the confines of a single street.

Conclusion

As the sun sets over the Maas River and the city lights illuminate Rotterdam's modern skyline, one cannot help but marvel at the transformation this city has undergone. Rotterdam, once synonymous with wartime destruction, has emerged as a testament to the power of human ingenuity and the indomitable spirit of renewal.

In the modern marvels of Rotterdam, one witnesses not only architectural audacity but also a city that has reinvented itself with a forward-thinking vision. The skyline, adorned with cable-stayed bridges, tilted cubes, and towering complexes, is a symbol of Rotterdam's determination to rise above its historical challenges and embrace the possibilities of the future.

So, as you navigate the sleek streets and riverbanks of Rotterdam, let the modernity envelop you, inspire you, and invite you to witness a city that has not just rebuilt itself but has forged a new identity—one that proudly wears the mantle of innovation, resilience, and progress. In Rotterdam, the modern marvels are not merely structures; they are testaments to the unwavering spirit of a city that continues to shape its destiny with each architectural innovation and urban endeavor.

The Hague - Royal Elegance

In the heart of the Netherlands, where history converges with politics and regal elegance permeates the atmosphere, The Hague stands as a city that exudes sophistication and cultural richness. Often referred to as the political capital of the Netherlands, The Hague transcends its administrative role, offering visitors a glimpse into a world where royal palaces, prestigious museums, and stately avenues converge to create an ambiance of timeless elegance.

Historical Tapestry

The history of The Hague is woven with threads of regal intrigue and political significance. As the seat of the Dutch government and the official residence of the Dutch monarch, The Hague has played a pivotal role in shaping the nation's destiny. Its roots trace back to the 13th century when Count Floris IV of Holland established a hunting lodge in the dense woodlands that would later become The Hague.

The Binnenhof, a medieval castle turned political complex, is the epicenter of The Hague's historical narrative. Surrounded by a tranquil lake, this architectural ensemble comprises the Ridderzaal (Knight's Hall) and the Hall of the Knights, serving as the backdrop for the annual State Opening of Parliament. The Binnenhof stands as a living testament to the city's medieval origins and its continued role as a hub of political activity.

Adjacent to the Binnenhof, the Mauritshuis Museum adds a cultural layer to The Hague's historical fabric. Housed in a 17th-century mansion built for John Maurice, Prince of Nassau-Siegen, the museum showcases an exquisite collection of Dutch Golden Age paintings. Works by Vermeer, Rembrandt, and other luminaries grace the museum's walls, providing visitors with a glimpse into the artistic legacy that flourished during this period.

Royal Residences

The Hague's regal elegance is further accentuated by the presence of royal residences that dot the cityscape. No visit to The Hague is complete without a journey to Noordeinde Palace, the official working palace of King Willem-Alexander. Nestled in the heart of the city, this 16th-century palace serves as the monarch's workplace and is often the backdrop for official ceremonies and events.

Huis ten Bosch, another royal residence located in The Hague, serves as the official residence of King Willem-Alexander and his family. Surrounded by lush gardens, this palace is an architectural jewel that embodies classical elegance. While the interiors are private, the meticulously landscaped gardens are occasionally open to the public, providing a glimpse into the royal aesthetic.

Cultural Enclaves

The Hague's cultural tapestry extends beyond regal residences to embrace a vibrant cultural scene. The Escher in Het Paleis museum, housed in the former Winter Palace of Queen Emma, celebrates the mind-bending works of Dutch graphic artist M.C. Escher. The museum's collection spans Escher's early sketches to his iconic optical illusion prints, creating an immersive experience that transcends traditional artistic boundaries.

For those seeking a deeper connection with history, the Gemeentemuseum Den Haag is a treasure trove of artistic and historical artifacts. This expansive museum, designed by architect H.P. Berlage, houses a diverse collection that ranges from the decorative arts to modern and contemporary masterpieces. The museum's commitment to innovation is evident in its design and curation, making it a must-visit destination for art enthusiasts.

Historical Enigma - The Peace Palace

The Peace Palace, an architectural marvel set amidst The Hague's urban landscape, stands as a symbol of the city's commitment to diplomacy and global peace. Constructed at the turn of the 20th century, the Peace Palace houses the International Court of Justice, the Permanent Court of Arbitration, and the renowned Peace Palace Library.

The Peace Palace, designed by French architect Louis Marie Cordonnier, is a harmonious blend of architectural styles, incorporating elements of Neo-Renaissance and Neo-Gothic design. The Great Hall of Justice, adorned with symbolic imagery and stained glass windows, is a testament to the ideals of international cooperation and conflict resolution.

The Peace Palace Library, with its vast collection of legal literature and documents, serves as a global resource for scholars, diplomats, and jurists. The Peace Palace, with its tranquil gardens and solemn halls, invites contemplation on the complexities of international relations and the pursuit of a more harmonious world.

Royal Parks and Gardens

The Hague's elegance extends to its meticulously landscaped parks and gardens, providing residents and visitors with serene retreats within the bustling city. The Paleistuin, or Palace Garden, adjacent to Noordeinde Palace, is a tranquil oasis featuring geometrically arranged flower beds, meandering paths, and classical sculptures. This historical garden, originally designed in the 17th century, offers a serene escape and a glimpse into the city's regal past.

Clive Square, known locally as the "Koningin Emmapark," is a charming green space named after Queen Emma. This park, with its picturesque pond and carefully manicured lawns, provides a peaceful respite for those seeking a moment of tranquility within the city.

The Scheveningen district, with its expansive beach and iconic pier, is a testament to The Hague's diverse offerings. The Scheveningen Pier, originally built in the late 19th century, has evolved into a modern entertainment complex with panoramic views of the North Sea. The nearby Scheveningen beach invites residents and tourists alike to enjoy seaside strolls, water sports, and the vibrant atmosphere of beachside cafes and restaurants.

International Flavor

As a city with a significant expatriate population and a strong diplomatic presence, The Hague's cultural palette is enriched by a diversity of influences. The International Zone, home to numerous embassies and international organizations, adds a cosmopolitan flair to the city. The iconic Europol headquarters, characterized by its distinctive globe-like structure, stands as a symbol of The Hague's role in global governance.

The International Court of Justice, housed within the Peace Palace, underscores The Hague's commitment to international law and justice. As the principal judicial organ of the United Nations, the court adjudicates disputes between states and offers a forum for peaceful resolution on the global stage.

Historical Enclaves - Statenkwartier and Archipelbuurt

The Statenkwartier and Archipelbuurt neighborhoods are historical enclaves within The Hague that encapsulate the city's architectural and cultural diversity. These districts, characterized by tree-lined streets, elegant townhouses, and a mix of architectural styles, offer a glimpse into The Hague's residential charm.

The Gemeentemuseum Den Haag, located in the Statenkwartier neighborhood, is not only a cultural gem but also an architectural masterpiece. Designed by H.P. Berlage, this museum, with its distinctive red brick facade and expressive use of geometric shapes, is an embodiment of the Art Nouveau movement.

The Archipelbuurt, known for its 19th-century architecture and leafy avenues, provides a tranquil residential setting. The Mesdag Collection, housed in the former residence of artist Hendrik Willem Mesdag, offers an intimate view of 19th-century Dutch art and the personal collection of the Mesdag family.

Culinary Journey

The culinary scene in The Hague mirrors the city's sophistication and international character. The Plein and Grote Markt squares, surrounded by cafes, bistros, and restaurants, are culinary hubs where residents and visitors can savor a diverse array of international cuisines. The historic Plein, with its outdoor terraces and views of the Binnenhof, offers an enchanting setting for al fresco dining.

For those seeking an epicurean adventure, the Denneweg, one of The Hague's oldest streets, beckons with a myriad of dining options. From fine dining establishments to cozy cafes, this historic street invites food enthusiasts to embark on a culinary journey through diverse flavors and gastronomic experiences.

Conclusion

In The Hague, the echoes of royal elegance, political gravitas, and cultural richness converge to create a city that embodies the essence of regal sophistication. Whether strolling through the manicured gardens of royal palaces, exploring the hallowed halls of diplomatic institutions, or savoring the diverse flavors of international cuisine, visitors to The Hague are immersed in an ambiance that transcends time.

The Hague's royal elegance is not merely a historical relic but a living, breathing facet of the city's identity. It is evident in the regal residences that grace the cityscape, the cultural enclaves that celebrate artistic expression, and the diplomatic forums that uphold principles of international cooperation.

As one navigates the streets of The Hague, from the historic Binnenhof to the tranquil parks and bustling squares, the city reveals itself as a destination where royal elegance is not a relic of the past but a dynamic force that shapes the present. In The Hague, every step is a journey through history, diplomacy, and the enduring elegance that defines this city at the crossroads of tradition and modernity.

Utrecht - Dom Tower and Beyond

Nestled along the banks of the Old Rhine River, the city of Utrecht emerges as a timeless tableau of history, culture, and architectural splendor. With its roots reaching back to Roman times, Utrecht stands as one of the oldest cities in the Netherlands, boasting a rich tapestry of medieval charm, vibrant canals, and a skyline dominated by the iconic Dom Tower. Beyond its historical landmarks, Utrecht invites visitors to explore a city where the past and present seamlessly intertwine, creating an atmosphere of cultural richness and intellectual vigor.

Historical Foundations

Utrecht's origins are intertwined with the Roman conquest of the Low Countries in the 1st century BCE. The settlement of Traiectum, established at the site of present-day Utrecht, served as a river crossing along the Rhine. Over the centuries, Utrecht evolved into a hub of religious and cultural significance, becoming the ecclesiastical center of the Netherlands.

The Dom Tower, an emblematic structure that defines Utrecht's skyline, stands as a testament to the city's medieval legacy. Construction of the tower began in the 14th century as part of the Utrecht Cathedral (Domkerk), a grand Gothic masterpiece. The Dom Tower, soaring to a height of 112 meters, remains the tallest church tower in the Netherlands, offering panoramic views that extend to the surrounding city and beyond.

The Domplein - A Historic Heart

The Domplein, the square surrounding the Dom Tower and the remnants of the incomplete cathedral nave, serves as the historical heart of Utrecht. As visitors enter the square, they are transported through time, surrounded by architectural remnants that tell the tale of Utrecht's medieval past.

The Domkerk, once a grand cathedral, now stands as a poignant reminder of the city's tumultuous history. The nave, destroyed in a 1674 storm, creates an open space within the Domplein, where visitors can meander through the hauntingly beautiful Pandhof garden and explore the archaeological remains of the original cathedral.

Adjacent to the Domkerk, the Domtoren Museum provides insights into the tower's construction, the history of Utrecht, and the significance of the cathedral complex. The museum's exhibits, ranging from medieval artifacts to architectural models, offer a comprehensive exploration of Utrecht's cultural and historical roots.

Dom Tower Ascent - A Panoramic Perspective

For the adventurous, a climb to the top of the Dom Tower promises a breathtaking panorama of Utrecht and its surroundings. The ascent involves navigating a narrow spiral staircase that winds its way through the tower's interior. As visitors ascend, they are treated to glimpses of the tower's bells, intricate Gothic architecture, and the city unfolding below.

Reaching the top, the reward is an unparalleled view that stretches across Utrecht's historic center, the meandering canals, and the verdant Dutch landscape. On a clear day, the vista extends to the distant horizons, providing a visual journey through the centuries and a profound appreciation for Utrecht's architectural marvels.

Canals and Waterways - Utrecht's Lifelines

Utrecht's canal network, although not as extensive as Amsterdam's, adds a distinctive charm to the cityscape. The Oudegracht, or Old Canal, serves as Utrecht's central waterway, lined with picturesque wharfs and historic buildings. As the sun sets, the waterside cafes and restaurants along the Oudegracht come alive, creating a romantic ambiance that is quintessentially Utrecht.

The unique feature of the Oudegracht is its subterranean wharfs, known as werfkelders. These cellar spaces, originally used for storage and trade, have been repurposed into trendy cafes, boutiques, and galleries. Walking along the quays, visitors can peer into the subterranean world, where the foundations of Utrecht's medieval structures are juxtaposed with contemporary urban life.

Cultural Flourish - Utrecht's Museums

Utrecht's cultural landscape extends beyond its historic core to encompass a diverse array of museums that celebrate art, history, and intellectual inquiry. The Centraal Museum, situated near the Domplein, stands as a cultural hub that spans centuries of artistic expression. From medieval religious art to contemporary Dutch design, the museum's collection offers a comprehensive journey through Utrecht's cultural evolution.

The Museum Catharijneconvent, located in a former monastery, is dedicated to the history of Christian art and culture in the Netherlands. Its exhibits, ranging from medieval manuscripts to religious artifacts, provide insights into the role of Utrecht as a center of ecclesiastical influence.

For those with a penchant for modern and contemporary art, the Miffy Museum (Nijntje Museum) pays homage to the beloved children's character created by Utrecht artist Dick Bruna. The museum's interactive exhibits engage visitors of all ages, making it a delightful destination for families.

Academic Legacy - Utrecht University

Utrecht's intellectual vitality is exemplified by the presence of Utrecht University, one of the oldest and most prestigious universities in the Netherlands. Founded in 1636, the university has been a cradle of learning, producing Nobel laureates, influential scholars, and contributing to advancements in various fields.

The university's historical Academiegebouw, with its distinctive bell tower, is a symbol of academic tradition. As visitors walk through the university's grounds, they are surrounded by centuries-old lecture halls, libraries, and courtyards that resonate with the pursuit of knowledge.

Utrecht University's Botanic Gardens, established in the 17th century, offer a serene escape within the city. The gardens showcase a diverse collection of plant species, including rare and exotic varieties, creating a living tapestry of biodiversity and horticultural fascination.

Neude Square - A Cultural Hub

The Neude Square, a bustling city square surrounded by cafes, bookshops, and cultural institutions, serves as a contemporary focal point within Utrecht. The square's historic allure is enhanced by the presence of the Neude Church, a former medieval parish church that has undergone various transformations over the centuries.

Today, the Neude Square is a hub of cultural activity, hosting events, markets, and festivals throughout the year. The square's vibrant atmosphere, with its lively terraces and eclectic shops, reflects Utrecht's modern spirit while maintaining a connection to its historical roots.

Innovation and Exploration - TivoliVredenburg

Utrecht's commitment to innovation and cultural exploration is epitomized by TivoliVredenburg, a contemporary music complex that marries architectural boldness with a diverse musical program. The complex, situated near Utrecht's central station, features multiple concert halls and spaces, each designed to offer acoustically refined experiences.

TivoliVredenburg's eclectic programming spans classical music, contemporary pop, jazz, and electronic genres, catering to a diverse audience. The complex's striking architectural design, with its interconnected volumes and reflective surfaces, adds a modern aesthetic to Utrecht's skyline, symbolizing the city's embrace of cultural dynamism.

Culinary Enclaves - Utrecht's Gastronomic Delights

Utrecht's culinary scene, influenced by its historical and multicultural character, offers a delectable array of dining experiences. The Twijnstraat, one of Utrecht's oldest streets, is a gastronomic enclave where specialty shops, bakeries, and restaurants beckon with a blend of traditional Dutch flavors and international influences.

The Stadskasteel Oudaen, a medieval castle turned brewery and restaurant, invites visitors to savor both culinary and historical delights. The castle's atmospheric setting, with its vaulted ceilings and ancient stone walls, creates a unique backdrop for enjoying locally brewed beers and inventive dishes.

As night falls, Utrecht's canalside restaurants and cafes along the Oudegracht come alive, offering a picturesque setting for al fresco dining. The city's culinary diversity, from Dutch classics to international cuisine, ensures that every palate finds satisfaction within Utrecht's charming streets.

Conclusion

Utrecht, with its medieval charm, iconic Dom Tower, and dynamic cultural scene, beckons visitors into a city where history and modernity coalesce seamlessly. Whether ascending the heights of the Dom Tower for panoramic views, wandering along the historic canals, or delving into the intellectual vibrancy of Utrecht University, every step is a journey through the layers of a city that has shaped Dutch history and culture.

In Utrecht, the past is not relegated to museums and monuments; it lives within the cobblestone streets, the canal reflections, and the architectural wonders that define the city. As the bells of the Dom Tower resonate over the rooftops and the canalside cafes hum with activity, Utrecht invites travelers to partake in a timeless exploration—one that transcends centuries and leaves an indelible mark on the cultural canvas of the Netherlands.

Giethoorn - The Venice of the North

Nestled in the tranquil province of Overijssel, amidst a patchwork of meadows and canals, Giethoorn emerges as a picturesque haven that transcends the ordinary. Aptly nicknamed the "Venice of the North," this idyllic village invites visitors to step into a world where the pace of life is dictated by the gentle lapping of canal waters and the rhythmic stroke of punting poles against the riverbed. Giethoorn, with its car-free waterways, thatched-roof cottages, and blooming gardens, is a testament to the harmonious coexistence of nature and human ingenuity.

Canal Tapestry - Giethoorn's Liquid Streets

At the heart of Giethoorn's allure lies its unique canal network, which serves as both thoroughfare and centerpiece. The village is crisscrossed by a myriad of canals, each flanked by charming cottages and adorned with arched wooden bridges. The tranquility that envelopes Giethoorn is not only a result of its car-free status but also a product of the silent gliding of boats along its liquid streets.

The primary mode of transportation in Giethoorn is the punt, a flat-bottomed boat propelled by a long pole. Visitors, whether locals or tourists, can navigate the canals at a leisurely pace, meandering through the waterways that weave through the village like a watery labyrinth. The absence of motorized vehicles transforms the canals into serene passageways, allowing the natural sounds of rustling leaves and birdsong to fill the air.

Thatched-Roof Charm - Architectural Elegance

Giethoorn's architectural aesthetic is defined by the quintessential charm of thatched-roof cottages, each a visual ode to traditional Dutch architecture. The cottages, adorned with vibrant gardens and often accompanied by small wooden bridges, exude a timeless elegance that seamlessly integrates with the natural surroundings.

The thatched roofs, a nod to centuries-old building techniques, not only add to the village's visual allure but also serve practical purposes.

Thatching, with its natural insulation properties, ensures that the interiors remain cool in summer and warm in winter. As visitors stroll along Giethoorn's narrow footpaths or cruise its canals, they are enveloped by the warmth of these charming dwellings, each telling a story of craftsmanship passed down through generations.

Floral Splendor - Gardens and Greenery

Giethoorn's commitment to natural beauty extends beyond its architectural gems to encompass the blooming gardens that punctuate the landscape. In spring and summer, vibrant flowers cascade over cottage fences, creating a kaleidoscope of colors that mirrors the diversity of the village itself. Residents take pride in cultivating their gardens, transforming them into miniature oases that complement the rustic charm of Giethoorn.

Wandering through the village, visitors encounter not only meticulously tended flowerbeds but also lush greenery that flourishes along the canals. Weeping willows gracefully dip their branches into the water, creating a poetic interplay between earth and liquid. As the seasons change, Giethoorn's gardens evolve, offering a different yet equally enchanting perspective with each visit.

Historical Footprints - De Oude Aarde and Museum Giethoorn 't Olde Maat Uus

Giethoorn, despite its quaint appearance, carries within it a rich tapestry of history and cultural heritage. De Oude Aarde, or The Old Earth, is a museum and shop that delves into the world of minerals and fossils. Founded in 1969, this unique establishment showcases an extensive collection of gemstones, crystals, and prehistoric artifacts. Visitors can explore the geological wonders of the Earth, acquiring a deeper appreciation for the natural forces that have shaped our planet.

Museum Giethoorn 't Olde Maat Uus, nestled along the village's waterways, offers a glimpse into the agricultural traditions of the region. Housed in a historic farmhouse, the museum recreates the daily life of a Giethoorn family in the early 20th century. From traditional farming implements to vintage interiors, the exhibits provide a nostalgic journey back in time, illustrating the resilience and resourcefulness of the village's inhabitants.

Culinary Delights - Waterside Dining and Local Fare

Giethoorn's culinary scene is a delightful blend of waterside dining and locally sourced fare. Restaurants and cafes along the canals offer a unique dining experience where patrons can savor a meal while watching boats glide by. The atmospheric charm of these waterside establishments, often adorned with flower-filled window boxes, enhances the gastronomic journey through Giethoorn.

Local cuisine in Giethoorn mirrors the village's connection to its natural surroundings. Freshly caught fish from the canals, locally produced cheeses, and farm-fresh vegetables find their way onto menus, creating a culinary tapestry that celebrates the flavors of the region. Whether indulging in a leisurely meal at a waterside terrace or sampling artisanal treats from local markets, visitors are treated to an authentic taste of Giethoorn's culinary heritage.

Festivals and Celebrations - Embracing Tradition

Giethoorn's community spirit is exemplified by its festive traditions and local celebrations. The annual Giethoorn International Jazz Festival, held against the backdrop of the village's waterways, transforms the serene setting into a vibrant stage for jazz enthusiasts from around the world. The festival, which has become a cherished tradition, adds a musical dimension to Giethoorn's cultural landscape.

During the summer months, the Giethoornse Gondelvaart, or the Giethoorn Canal Parade, brings the village to life with illuminated boats floating along the canals. Locals decorate their punts with creative themes and colorful lights, transforming the waterways into a spectacle of light and imagination. The parade, a testament to the community's creativity and camaraderie, has become a beloved event that draws visitors and participants alike.

Nature Reserves - De Wieden and Weerribben

Surrounding Giethoorn are the nature reserves of De Wieden and Weerribben, expansive wetlands that beckon nature enthusiasts and outdoor adventurers. These protected areas, characterized by reed beds, open waters, and diverse flora and fauna, provide a counterpoint to the tranquility of Giethoorn's canals.

De Wieden, with its interconnected waterways, is a haven for birdwatchers, offering opportunities to spot a variety of waterfowl, including herons and kingfishers. Weerribben, known for its peat bogs and fen vegetation, provides hiking and cycling trails that lead through a mosaic of landscapes, revealing the region's natural diversity.

Conclusion

Giethoorn, the Venice of the North, transcends the conventional with its car-free canals, thatched-roof cottages, and blooming gardens. It is a village where time seems to slow down, allowing visitors to immerse themselves in the gentle rhythms of punting poles and the natural serenity that envelops the landscape.

In Giethoorn, the union of human craftsmanship and natural beauty is palpable, creating an atmosphere that is both nostalgic and timeless. As visitors punt along the canals, stroll through flower-lined pathways, and indulge in waterside dining, they become part of a living postcard—one that captures the essence of a village where the ordinary becomes extraordinary, and every corner reveals a story of tradition, community, and the harmonious dance between humanity and nature.

Haarlem - Art and History

Nestled on the banks of the Spaarne River, Haarlem stands as a testament to the intricate interplay between art and history. As one of the oldest cities in the Netherlands, Haarlem weaves a narrative that unfolds through cobblestone streets, historic architecture, and a vibrant cultural scene. From the iconic St. Bavo's Cathedral to the illustrious Frans Hals Museum, Haarlem invites visitors to embark on a journey through the annals of Dutch artistry and the rich tapestry of its historical legacy.

Historical Foundations

Haarlem's roots reach deep into the annals of Dutch history, with evidence of human habitation dating back to prehistoric times. However, it was during the medieval period that Haarlem began to flourish as a bustling market town and trading center. The city's strategic location along waterways contributed to its economic prosperity, while its fortified walls and gates reflected the importance of defense in a tumultuous historical landscape.

The Grote Markt, Haarlem's central square, remains a focal point where history converges with contemporary life. Surrounding the square, historic buildings with stepped gables and ornate facades speak to the city's architectural evolution. The Grote Kerk, or St. Bavo's Cathedral, dominates the skyline, its towering spire a testament to the city's ecclesiastical significance.

St. Bavo's Cathedral - Ecclesiastical Splendor

St. Bavo's Cathedral, a Gothic masterpiece that traces its origins to the 14th century, is an architectural gem that encapsulates Haarlem's religious heritage. The cathedral's soaring spire, reaching over 70 meters in height, serves as a beacon visible from afar. As visitors enter the cathedral, they are greeted by a sense of grandeur, with tall vaulted ceilings, intricate stained glass windows, and ornate chapels that reflect the city's devotion to its religious history.

One of St. Bavo's Cathedral's most renowned features is the Müller organ, an instrument that has gained international acclaim for its craftsmanship and musical capabilities. The organ, dating back to the 18th century, has resonated within the cathedral's walls, filling the sacred space with harmonies that evoke a sense of transcendence.

Adjacent to the cathedral, the Grote Kerk Square provides a tranquil oasis within the city. Flanked by historic buildings and cafes, the square offers a space for reflection and appreciation of Haarlem's architectural and cultural heritage.

Frans Hals Museum - Artistic Legacy

Haarlem's cultural tapestry is intricately woven with the brushstrokes of the renowned Golden Age painter Frans Hals. The Frans Hals Museum, named in honor of the masterful artist, is a repository of Dutch Golden Age paintings and a celebration of Haarlem's artistic legacy.

The museum, housed in a complex of historic buildings, presents an extensive collection of works by Frans Hals and his contemporaries. The portraits and genre paintings on display provide a vivid snapshot of life during the 17th century, capturing the spirit and dynamism of the Dutch Golden Age. Frans Hals' skillful use of light and his ability to capture the essence of his subjects are evident in works such as "The Laughing Cavalier" and "The Banquet of the Officers of the St. George Militia Company."

Beyond Frans Hals, the museum's collection includes pieces by other Dutch masters such as Jacob van Ruisdael, Jan Steen, and Pieter Saenredam. Each canvas tells a story of artistic innovation and cultural flourishing, inviting visitors to delve into the nuances of Dutch artistry during this transformative period.

Historical Enclaves - Hofjes and Windmills

Haarlem's charm extends beyond its central squares and museums to encompass hidden gems known as hofjes. These almshouses, enclosed within serene courtyards, were established during the medieval and Renaissance periods to provide housing for the elderly and needy. Today, these hofjes offer a glimpse into Haarlem's historical social welfare initiatives and serve as peaceful retreats within the urban landscape.

The Hofje van Bakenes, dating back to the 14th century, is one such enclave that transports visitors to a bygone era. Its quaint houses, surrounding a central garden, evoke a sense of tranquility and historical continuity. As visitors stroll through the hofjes, they are immersed in the architectural aesthetics of Haarlem's past and the benevolent intentions that gave rise to these hidden havens.

The windmills that dot the outskirts of Haarlem stand as iconic symbols of Dutch ingenuity and resourcefulness. Molen de Adriaan, a reconstructed industrial windmill, offers panoramic views of the city and the surrounding landscapes. Originally built in 1779, the mill was destroyed by fire in 1932 but was meticulously reconstructed in the late 20th century. Today, Molen de Adriaan stands as a testament to Haarlem's industrial heritage and its commitment to preserving historical landmarks.

Teylers Museum - Art, Science, and Enlightenment

Teylers Museum, nestled along the Spaarne River, is a cultural institution that transcends traditional boundaries. Established in 1784, the museum embodies the ideals of the Enlightenment, seamlessly integrating art and science within its hallowed halls. As the oldest museum in the Netherlands, Teylers holds a unique position as a custodian of knowledge and a testament to the intellectual pursuits that defined the 18th century.

The Oval Room, with its neoclassical design, houses a diverse collection of art and scientific instruments. Visitors can explore cabinets of curiosities, marvel at fossil specimens, and admire paintings by artists such as Michelangelo and Rembrandt. Teylers Museum, with its commitment to the intersection of art and knowledge, invites contemplation on the interconnectedness of human creativity and intellectual exploration.

Culinary Delights - Gourmet Haarlem

Haarlem's culinary scene reflects the city's sophistication and diverse influences. The Grote Markt and its surrounding streets are culinary hubs where cafes, bistros, and restaurants offer a spectrum of gastronomic delights. Visitors can savor traditional Dutch dishes, explore international cuisines, and indulge in gourmet experiences that highlight the city's culinary creativity.

The Vishuisje, a historic fishmonger's shop, pays homage to Haarlem's maritime heritage. With its charming blue-and-white facade, the Vishuisje has been serving fresh seafood to locals and visitors for over a century. Haarlem's markets, such as the Botermarkt and the Haarlemmermeerstraat, provide opportunities to sample local cheeses, artisanal treats, and seasonal produce.

The city's commitment to quality dining is exemplified by its Michelin-starred restaurants, where innovative chefs showcase the finest ingredients and culinary craftsmanship. Gourmet Haarlem, with its fusion of tradition and modernity, offers a delectable journey for discerning palates.

City Parks and Outdoor Retreats

Haarlem's commitment to green spaces adds a refreshing dimension to its urban landscape. The Haarlemmerhout, one of the oldest public parks in the Netherlands, provides a sprawling retreat where residents and visitors can escape the urban bustle. The park's majestic avenues, shaded by centuries-old trees, invite leisurely strolls and moments of repose.

The Bolwerken, a network of defensive ramparts and moats, offers a unique blend of history and nature. Today, these green enclaves provide recreational spaces where locals engage in sports, picnics, and moments of relaxation. Haarlem's dedication to preserving and enhancing its green spaces underscores the city's commitment to balancing urban life with natural beauty.

Festivals and Events - Celebrating Culture

Haarlem's cultural vibrancy comes to the forefront during its festivals and events, which celebrate the city's artistic heritage and contemporary creativity. The Haarlem Jazz & More Festival, held annually in August, transforms the city into a musical haven, with open-air performances, jam sessions, and a lively atmosphere that echoes through its historic streets.

The Haarlemse Lakenfeesten, or Haarlem Cloth Festival, pays homage to the city's historical textile industry. This multi-day event, featuring parades, markets, and cultural activities, invites locals and visitors to partake in the festivities and immerse themselves in Haarlem's historical and cultural richness.

Conclusion

Haarlem, with its art-laden museums, historical landmarks, and dynamic cultural scene, stands as a testament to the enduring connection between artistic expression and the tapestry of human history. Whether admiring the intricate architecture of St. Bavo's Cathedral, exploring the brushstrokes of Frans Hals, or wandering through hidden hofjes, every step in Haarlem is a journey through time and creativity.

In Haarlem, the city's past and present converge to create an environment where artistry is not confined to canvas but is woven into the very fabric of urban life. As the Spaarne River meanders through the city and the bells of St. Bavo's Cathedral resonate in the air, Haarlem invites visitors to partake in a cultural symphony—one that harmonizes the echoes of centuries past with the vibrant pulse of contemporary expression.

Delft - Pottery and Palaces

Nestled in the southwestern reaches of the Netherlands, Delft emerges as a city that seamlessly marries artistic ingenuity with historical grandeur. Renowned for its iconic blue and white pottery, historic canals, and regal palaces, Delft invites visitors to traverse its cobblestone streets and immerse themselves in a cultural tapestry that spans centuries. From the masterpieces of the Royal Delft factory to the solemn beauty of the Old Church, Delft stands as a testament to the enduring elegance of Dutch craftsmanship and the rich history that shaped its destiny.

Historical Roots and Cityscape

Delft's origins can be traced back to the 11th century when it began as a small settlement along the Gantel River. Over the centuries, it evolved into a hub of commerce and industry, its canals and waterways playing a vital role in the transportation of goods. Delft's historical roots are deeply intertwined with the rise of the Dutch Golden Age, marked by economic prosperity, artistic flourishing, and the establishment of the Dutch East India Company.

The cityscape of Delft reflects its rich history, with medieval architecture harmonizing with later styles. The Markt, Delft's central square, serves as a vibrant focal point surrounded by historic buildings and the imposing Nieuwe Kerk (New Church). As visitors meander through the Markt and its adjacent streets, they encounter a visual journey through the centuries, from the Renaissance facades to the elegant gables that line the canals.

Royal Delft - Blue and White Masterpieces

Delft's association with distinctive blue and white pottery dates back to the 17th century when artisans sought to emulate the prized Chinese porcelain that was highly coveted during the Dutch Golden Age. Royal Delft, established in 1653, stands as a testament to this enduring tradition of craftsmanship.

visitors to Royal Delft are welcomed into a world where precision meets artistry. The factory's craftsmen meticulously shape clay into delicate forms, transforming them into exquisite pieces adorned with intricate blue and white designs. The process of hand-painting, glazing, and firing each piece follows time-honored techniques, preserving the authenticity of Delftware.

The showroom at Royal Delft offers a captivating display of the company's creations, from classic vases and tiles to contemporary interpretations of the traditional art form. Exploring the history of Delftware within the walls of Royal Delft provides a deeper appreciation for the craftsmanship that has defined the city for centuries.

Nieuwe Kerk - A Royal Resting Place

Delft's skyline is crowned by the Nieuwe Kerk, a towering Gothic church that has played a pivotal role in the city's history. Construction of the Nieuwe Kerk began in the 14th century, and its grandeur was enhanced over the years, culminating in the completion of its iconic spire in the 17th century.

One of the most significant aspects of the Nieuwe Kerk is its association with the Dutch royal family. The church serves as the final resting place for members of the House of Orange-Nassau, the royal dynasty of the Netherlands. The ornate mausoleum of William of Orange, known as the Father of the Fatherland, is a focal point within the church. The solemn beauty of the Nieuwe Kerk, with its stained glass windows and impressive organ, provides a poignant backdrop to the historical narratives etched into its walls.

Prinsenhof - Palace of History

The Prinsenhof, a former convent turned princely residence, is a testament to Delft's regal legacy. Originally built in the 15th century, the Prinsenhof gained historical significance during the Dutch Revolt when it served as the residence of William of Orange. It was within these walls that William of Orange was assassinated in 1584, making the Prinsenhof a site of national importance.

Today, the Prinsenhof has been transformed into a museum that chronicles the history of the Netherlands and the life of William of Orange. The museum's exhibits include artifacts from the Dutch Golden Age, paintings, and the bullet holes that mark the spot where William of Orange met his untimely end. The tranquil gardens surrounding the Prinsenhof provide a serene retreat, inviting visitors to reflect on the pivotal moments that unfolded within its historic confines.

Oude Kerk - Timeless Tranquility

The Oude Kerk, or Old Church, stands as Delft's oldest parish church, its foundations dating back to the 13th century. As one of the city's most cherished landmarks, the Oude Kerk offers a haven of tranquility amidst the bustling streets of Delft.

The interior of the Oude Kerk is a testament to the passage of time, with its timber roof, medieval stained glass windows, and a majestic pipe organ that dates back to the 18th century. The church's iconic leaning tower, known as the Scheve Jan, adds a touch of whimsy to the city's skyline. The Oude Kerk's serene ambiance provides a space for contemplation and appreciation of Delft's enduring spiritual and architectural heritage.

Canals and Bridges - Delft's Liquid Threads

Delft's canals, though less expansive than those in Amsterdam, contribute to the city's charm and functionality. The Oude Delft, the oldest canal in the city, winds its way through the historic center, lined with picturesque houses, shops, and cafes. The canal's reflections add a poetic dimension to the city's aesthetic, especially during the twilight hours when the glow of streetlights is mirrored in the water.

The numerous bridges that span Delft's canals not only facilitate passage but also serve as vantage points for capturing the city's beauty. The Hoge Brug, a high arched bridge near the Markt, provides panoramic views of the Nieuwe Kerk and the surrounding historic buildings. Crossing Delft's canals, whether by foot or bike, offers glimpses into the city's architectural diversity and the interplay between water and urban life.

Delft University of Technology - Innovation and Education

Delft's commitment to innovation and education is epitomized by the presence of Delft University of Technology (TU Delft). Founded in 1842, TU Delft has evolved into a globally recognized institution known for its contributions to engineering, technology, and design.

The university's modern campus, with its sleek architecture and cutting-edge facilities, stands in contrast to the historical backdrop of the city. TU Delft's commitment to research and development is evident in its collaborations with industries, its emphasis on sustainable technologies, and its role in shaping the next generation of innovators. The Aula, TU Delft's ceremonial hall, is a striking example of architectural modernity within the city, symbolizing the convergence of tradition and progress.

Culinary Diversity - Gastronomic Explorations

Delft's culinary scene reflects the city's cosmopolitan character, with a diverse array of dining options that cater to both locals and visitors. The Beestenmarkt, a historic square surrounded by cafes and restaurants, serves as a culinary hub where patrons can enjoy al fresco dining while immersing themselves in the lively atmosphere.

Local markets, such as the Nieuwe Markt and the Brabantse Turfmarkt, provide opportunities to savor Dutch delicacies, artisanal cheeses, and fresh produce. Delft's eateries, ranging from traditional Dutch pubs to international cuisine, offer a gastronomic journey that complements the city's cultural richness.

Festivals and Celebrations - Cultural Revelry

Delft's festivals and celebrations add a festive dimension to the city's cultural calendar. The Delft Chamber Music Festival, held annually, transforms historic venues into stages for classical performances, attracting musicians and enthusiasts from around the world. The Delft Ceramica, a ceramics market, showcases the city's artistic heritage and contemporary innovations in pottery.

During Koningsdag, or King's Day, Delft joins the nationwide celebration with vibrant street markets, live music, and festivities that honor
the Dutch royal family. These cultural revelries bring the community together and infuse the city with a sense of joy and camaraderie.

Conclusion

Delft, with its blue and white pottery, regal palaces, and winding
canals, unfolds as a city where artistic mastery and historical grandeur
coalesce. Every step through its cobblestone streets is a journey through
time, from the bustling markets of the Dutch Golden Age to the innovations of Delft University of Technology. As visitors explore the masterpieces of Royal Delft, gaze upon the spire of the Nieuwe Kerk, or con-
template within the Prinsenhof's hallowed halls, they become part of a
narrative that spans centuries—a narrative where craftsmanship, culture,
and history converge to create the timeless allure of Delft.

Maastricht - Culinary Delights

In the southernmost reaches of the Netherlands, where the Meuse River gracefully winds its way through cobbled streets and historic squares, Maastricht emerges as a culinary haven that beckons gourmands and connoisseurs alike. This city, with its blend of medieval charm and cosmopolitan flair, offers a gastronomic journey that unfolds in Michelin-starred restaurants, vibrant markets, and welcoming cafes. From the aromatic stalls of the Markt to the innovative kitchens of renowned chefs, Maastricht invites visitors to savor the rich tapestry of flavors that define Dutch and international cuisines.

Historical Tapestry and Culinary Crossroads

Maastricht's culinary identity is deeply rooted in its historical tapestry, shaped by centuries of cultural exchange and influences from neighboring Belgium and Germany. As one of the oldest cities in the Netherlands, Maastricht's cobblestone streets and well-preserved medieval architecture provide a picturesque backdrop for culinary exploration.

The city's strategic location along ancient trade routes contributed to its status as a culinary crossroads, where ingredients, techniques, and flavors converged. Maastricht's culinary scene, vibrant and diverse, reflects this rich history, offering a fusion of traditional Dutch dishes and international gastronomic innovations.

Markt and Vrijthof - Culinary Epicenters

The Markt and Vrijthof, Maastricht's central squares, are culinary epicenters where the city's gastronomic pulse is most palpable. The Markt, surrounded by historic buildings and overlooked by the towering Stadhuis (City Hall), hosts a bustling market where vendors showcase fresh produce, artisanal cheeses, and regional specialties. The scent of freshly baked bread, the sight of vibrant fruits and vegetables, and the sounds of market vendors create an immersive experience that captivates the senses.

Vrijthof, a square framed by the iconic St. Servaas Basilica and St. John's Church, transforms into an open-air dining destination during the warmer months. Its terraces, adorned with umbrellas and surrounded by historic architecture, offer a charming setting for indulging in culinary delights while soaking in the atmosphere of this historic square.

Bouchon d'en Face - French Elegance in Maastricht

Maastricht's culinary diversity is exemplified by Bouchon d'en Face, a restaurant that channels the elegance of French cuisine within the heart of the city. Nestled in a historic building, this establishment combines traditional French flavors with a contemporary twist, creating a dining experience that is both refined and welcoming.

Bouchon d'en Face's menu, curated by skilled chefs, features dishes that showcase the finest ingredients sourced from local markets and international suppliers. From classic French staples such as coq au vin to innovative creations like foie gras with elderflower, each plate is a masterpiece that pays homage to culinary artistry. The restaurant's commitment to pairing exquisite flavors with an extensive wine selection enhances the gastronomic journey, making Bouchon d'en Face a destination for those seeking a taste of French elegance in Maastricht.

Dominicaner Bookstore - Culinary and Literary Fusion

In the heart of Maastricht, the Dominicaner Bookstore stands as a unique testament to the fusion of culinary and literary arts. Housed in a former Dominican church, this bookstore offers an immersive experience where patrons can explore an extensive collection of books while savoring artisanal coffee and pastries.

The bookstore's café, nestled among towering bookshelves and beneath the vaulted ceilings of the church, creates a tranquil ambiance for indulging in culinary delights amidst a literary landscape. The menu, inspired by the flavors of the region, features locally sourced ingredients and a selection of sweet and savory offerings. The Dominicaner Bookstore is not just a destination for book lovers but a haven where the pleasures of literature and gastronomy converge.

Taste of Maastricht - Culinary Walking Tours

To truly appreciate the depth and diversity of Maastricht's culinary scene, visitors can embark on a "Taste of Maastricht" culinary walking tour. These guided tours, led by local experts, take participants on a journey through the city's hidden culinary gems, from traditional markets to contemporary eateries.

The tour provides insights into Maastricht's culinary history, introduces participants to local producers and artisans, and offers tastings of regional specialties. Whether sampling Limburgse vlaai (a traditional fruit tart), savoring local cheeses, or experiencing the craftsmanship behind traditional stroopwafels, the "Taste of Maastricht" tours engage the senses and provide a holistic understanding of the city's culinary heritage.

Château Neercanne - Michelin-Starred Excellence

For those seeking a Michelin-starred dining experience, Château Neercanne stands as an epitome of culinary excellence in Maastricht. This historic château, surrounded by terraced gardens and overlooking the Jeker Valley, houses a restaurant that has earned prestigious Michelin stars for its commitment to gastronomic innovation.

Château Neercanne's culinary offerings reflect a marriage of classical French techniques with a modern and creative approach. The seasonal menu, curated by the talented kitchen team, showcases the finest local and international ingredients. Diners can indulge in meticulously crafted dishes such as lobster with caviar or Wagyu beef with truffle, each plate presenting a symphony of flavors and textures. The château's terraced gardens, where fruits, herbs, and edible flowers are cultivated, contribute to the restaurant's dedication to freshness and quality.

Bisschopsmolen - Traditional Dutch Delicacies

Maastricht's culinary landscape is enriched by Bisschopsmolen, a historic watermill turned bakery that has been producing traditional Dutch delicacies for centuries. Located along the Jeker River, this artisanal bakery preserves age-old baking techniques and recipes, offering patrons a taste of authentic Limburgse treats.

Bisschopsmolen is renowned for its vlaai, a traditional Limburgse pie filled with fruits, custard, or regional specialties such as rijstevlaai (rice pie). The bakery's commitment to using high-quality ingredients, combined with the charm of its historic setting, creates an experience that transports visitors to the heart of Dutch culinary tradition. The aroma of freshly baked goods and the visual allure of the watermill add to the sensory delight of a visit to Bisschopsmolen.

Café Sjiek - Local Flavors and Cozy Atmosphere

Café Sjiek, nestled within the historic Wyck district, embodies the essence of Maastricht's local flavors and warm hospitality. This beloved café, housed in a quaint corner building with a cozy interior, has become a go-to destination for both locals and visitors seeking a taste of authentic Limburgse cuisine.

The menu at Café Sjiek features a variety of dishes inspired by regional ingredients, with a focus on hearty and comforting fare. From Limburgse gehaktballen (meatballs) to zoervleis (sweet and sour stew), each dish reflects the culinary heritage of the region. The intimate ambiance, characterized by wooden furnishings and dim lighting, adds to the overall charm of Café Sjiek, making it a place where patrons can savor the essence of Maastricht's culinary traditions.

Maastricht Market - A Tapestry of Flavors

The Maastricht Market, held in the Markt square, is a vibrant tapestry of flavors that showcases the best of local and international produce. This open-air market, a longstanding tradition in the city, draws vendors from the surrounding region who present an array of fresh fruits, vegetables, cheeses, and artisanal products.

Wandering through the stalls of the Maastricht Market is a sensory experience that allows visitors to engage with the richness of Limburgse gastronomy. From pungent cheeses to fragrant herbs, the market offers a diverse palette of ingredients that inspire both home cooks and professional chefs. The lively atmosphere, punctuated by the calls of vendors and the vibrant colors of fresh produce, contributes to the dynamic energy of Maastricht's culinary scene.

Culinary Festivals - Celebrating Flavor

Maastricht's culinary calendar is punctuated by festivals and events that celebrate the city's diverse flavors and culinary creativity. The Preuvenemint, held annually in August, transforms the Vrijthof square into a sprawling culinary festival where attendees can sample dishes from a multitude of restaurants and vendors. This event, one of the largest open-air food festivals in the Netherlands, encapsulates the spirit of Maastricht's gastronomic scene.

The Rrrollend Maastricht Food Truck Festival adds a modern and dynamic flair to the city's culinary celebrations. This traveling food festival features a convoy of food trucks offering a diverse range of international cuisines, creating a lively and eclectic atmosphere that resonates with Maastricht's cosmopolitan character.

Conclusion

Maastricht, with its medieval charm and culinary diversity, emerges as a city where every dish is a testament to the region's rich gastronomic heritage. Whether indulging in the elegance of a Michelin-starred dining experience at Château Neercanne, savoring traditional Dutch treats at Bisschopsmolen, or exploring the vibrant stalls of the Maastricht Market, visitors are invited to embark on a culinary journey that transcends the boundaries of time and tradition.

In Maastricht, culinary delights are not merely sustenance; they are a celebration of culture, history, and the artistry of those who transform simple ingredients into culinary masterpieces. The city's gastronomic tapestry, woven with the threads of tradition and innovation, beckons all who seek to savor the flavors of Maastricht—a city where each meal is an invitation to partake in the timeless joy of shared experiences and exceptional cuisine.

National Parks - Nature's Beauty

Netherlands, a country renowned for its cultural heritage and historic cities, also boasts a remarkable tapestry of natural beauty preserved within its national parks. Despite its relatively modest size, the Netherlands is home to diverse ecosystems, wetlands, and landscapes that showcase the delicate balance between nature and human intervention. The national parks of the Netherlands invite visitors to explore pristine wilderness, meandering rivers, and flourishing flora and fauna, providing a sanctuary for both biodiversity and those seeking refuge from urban life.

Hoge Veluwe National Park - A Symphony of Forests and Sand Dunes

Hoge Veluwe National Park, nestled in the heart of the Netherlands, unfolds as a vast expanse of natural wonders where dense forests, expansive heaths, and shifting sand dunes create a harmonious symphony of landscapes. This national park, encompassing over 55 square kilometers, stands as a testament to the country's commitment to preserving its diverse ecosystems.

The landscape of Hoge Veluwe is characterized by the ancient woodlands of the Veluwe, where centuries-old oaks and beech trees create a dense canopy. Visitors can explore the park's network of walking and cycling trails, immersing themselves in the tranquility of the forested surroundings. The shifting sands, a unique feature of Hoge Veluwe, add an ethereal quality to the landscape, creating a dynamic interplay between nature and the elements.

The Kröller-Müller Museum, located within the park, further enhances the visitor's experience by combining art and nature. The museum, surrounded by sculpture gardens and open-air exhibits, houses an impressive collection of paintings by Van Gogh, Picasso, and other masters, providing a cultural complement to the natural beauty of Hoge Veluwe.

De Hoge Kempen National Park - Flanders' Green Heart

Straddling the border between the Netherlands and Belgium, De Hoge Kempen National Park is a verdant expanse that showcases the natural beauty of the Kempen region. Encompassing both sides of the border, this transboundary park is the largest national park in Flanders, Belgium, and the only national park in the Netherlands. De Hoge Kempen unfolds as a mosaic of landscapes, featuring heathlands, forests, and waterways that provide a haven for biodiversity.

The park's extensive network of hiking and cycling trails allows visitors to explore its diverse ecosystems, from the heathlands of Mechelse Heide to the lush woodlands of Station As. The landscape is punctuated by tranquil lakes and meandering streams, creating opportunities for birdwatching and wildlife observation. De Hoge Kempen National Park serves as a testament to the collaborative efforts between the Netherlands and Belgium in preserving and showcasing the natural treasures of the Kempen region.

Oostvaardersplassen - A Haven for Wetland Biodiversity

Oostvaardersplassen, situated in the reclaimed Flevoland polder, emerges as a haven for wetland biodiversity and a testament to the dynamic relationship between nature and human intervention. This unique nature reserve, once envisioned as an industrial area, has evolved into a thriving ecosystem that harbors diverse bird species, large herbivores, and an array of aquatic life.

The landscape of Oostvaardersplassen is characterized by expansive reed beds, marshes, and open waters. The reserve is home to a significant population of wild Konik horses, Heck cattle, and red deer, which contribute to the natural grazing dynamics of the ecosystem. Birdwatchers flock to Oostvaardersplassen to observe a multitude of avian species, including migratory birds that use the wetlands as a crucial stopover during their journeys.

Oostvaardersplassen exemplifies the Netherlands' innovative approach to conservation, where the delicate balance between natural processes and human management creates a landscape that mirrors the untamed beauty of the wild.

Drents-Friese Wold National Park - A Tapestry of Forests and Heathlands

Drents-Friese Wold National Park, spanning the provinces of Drenthe and Friesland, unfolds as a tapestry of ancient forests, expansive heathlands, and shifting sands. This diverse landscape, shaped by geological processes and human interaction, provides a refuge for a variety of plant and animal species.

The Aekingerzand, also known as the Kale Duinen, is a unique feature of Drents-Friese Wold, where shifting sands create an ever-changing mosaic of dunes and heathlands. The park's dense woodlands, including the majestic Boschoord and Terwisscha, invite visitors to explore a network of trails that wind through ancient oaks, birches, and Scots pines.

Drents-Friese Wold is a haven for outdoor enthusiasts, offering opportunities for hiking, cycling, and horseback riding. The park's diverse ecosystems, from the vibrant heathlands to the serene beech forests, contribute to its appeal as a natural sanctuary in the heart of the Netherlands.

Weerribben-Wieden National Park - Water Wonderland

Weerribben-Wieden National Park, located in the province of Overijssel, unfolds as a water wonderland where a network of lakes, canals, and wetlands creates a mosaic of aquatic habitats. This expansive wetland reserve is renowned for its picturesque landscapes, abundant birdlife, and a rich cultural history shaped by peat extraction.

The waterways of Weerribben-Wieden crisscross through reed beds, marshes, and floating islands, providing a haven for a diverse array of flora and fauna. Visitors can explore the park's intricate waterways by boat, canoe, or on foot, immersing themselves in the tranquility of the wetland environment.

The historic village of Giethoorn, often referred to as the "Venice of the North," is nestled within the boundaries of Weerribben-Wieden.

This charming village, with its thatched-roof cottages and wooden bridges, adds a cultural dimension to the park, inviting visitors to explore the interplay between human settlements and the surrounding wetlands.

Veluwezoom National Park - Veluwe's Crown Jewel

Veluwezoom National Park, situated on the eastern edge of the Veluwe, unfolds as the crown jewel of this ancient landscape. The park's diverse habitats, ranging from heathlands and sand dunes to dense woodlands, create a rich mosaic of ecosystems that support a wide variety of wildlife.

The Posbank, a prominent hill within Veluwezoom, offers panoramic views of the surrounding landscapes, with vibrant heather in hues of purple and pink during the late summer months. The park's extensive network of trails allows visitors to explore its diverse terrain, encountering ancient oak trees, grazing red deer, and the meandering IJssel River.

Veluwezoom National Park stands as a testament to the Veluwe's ecological significance and the efforts to preserve its natural heritage. The park's commitment to sustainable conservation practices ensures that future generations can continue to experience the untamed beauty of this ancient landscape.

Schiermonnikoog National Park - Island Serenity

Schiermonnikoog, the smallest inhabited Wadden Island, is a tranquil haven that unfolds as a national park where dunes, beaches, and tidal flats create a serene coastal landscape. Designated as a UNESCO World Heritage site, Schiermonnikoog National Park embodies the unique dynamics of the Wadden Sea and serves as a vital refuge for migratory birds.

The island's pristine beaches, including the expansive North Sea beach and the sheltered Westerstrand, offer opportunities for relaxation and exploration. Visitors can traverse the island on foot or by bicycle, encountering diverse habitats ranging from salt marshes to maritime forests.

Schiermonnikoog's commitment to sustainable tourism and conservation has led to the implementation of measures to protect its fragile ecosystems. The island's status as a car-free zone enhances the visitor's experience, allowing them to connect with nature in its purest form and contributing to the preservation of Schiermonnikoog's natural heritage.

Dwingelderveld National Park - A Heathland Retreat

Dwingelderveld National Park, located in the province of Drenthe, unfolds as a vast heathland retreat where expansive vistas, meandering streams, and ancient burial mounds create a landscape of timeless beauty. As the largest contiguous heathland in Western Europe, Dwingelderveld is a testament to the ecological significance of these unique ecosystems.

The park's diverse habitats include not only heathlands but also woodlands, wetlands, and drifting sand dunes. Visitors can explore the park's network of trails, encountering iconic species such as the European adder and the Dwingelderveld sheep, which play a crucial role in maintaining the balance of the heathland ecosystems.

Dwingelderveld National Park invites those seeking tranquility and a connection with nature to immerse themselves in the timeless beauty of its heathlands. The park's commitment to sustainable conservation practices ensures that these landscapes, with their vibrant heather blooms and the calls of ground-nesting birds, remain a sanctuary for generations to come.

Zuid-Kennemerland National Park - Dunes and Coastal Diversity

Zuid-Kennemerland National Park, situated along the North Sea coast, unfolds as a dynamic landscape where rolling dunes, coastal forests, and expansive beaches create a haven for biodiversity. This coastal gem, nestled between the cities of Haarlem and Zandvoort, provides a retreat for both nature enthusiasts and those seeking the therapeutic benefits of coastal landscapes.

The park's diverse ecosystems include shifting dunes, meandering waterways, and vibrant heathlands. Visitors can explore the park's trails, encountering iconic species such as European bison, Scottish Highland cattle, and the elusive European mink. The coastal area of Zuid-Kennemerland is a vital habitat for migratory birds, adding to the park's ecological significance.

The historic country estate of Elswout, located within the park, offers a cultural dimension to the visitor's experience. The estate's ornate gardens, historic buildings, and picturesque landscapes provide a tranquil setting for exploration and reflection.

Alde Feanen National Park - Friesland's Wetland Jewel

Alde Feanen National Park, situated in the province of Friesland, stands as a wetland jewel where a mosaic of lakes, peat bogs, and reed beds create a haven for waterfowl and aquatic life. This dynamic landscape, shaped by centuries of human interaction and the forces of nature, reflects the resilience of wetland ecosystems in the face of change.

The park's waterways, including the Princenhof Route and the wide-open spaces of the Alde Feanen, provide opportunities for boating, bird-watching, and exploration. Visitors can navigate the intricate network of canals and discover the rich biodiversity that thrives in the wetland environment.

Alde Feanen National Park is not only a sanctuary for nature but also a cultural landscape shaped by human activities such as peat extraction and traditional farming practices. The park's commitment to sustainable conservation ensures that this wetland jewel remains a vibrant and vital part of Friesland's natural and cultural heritage.

Oosterschelde National Park - Tidal Dynamics and Marine Life

Oosterschelde National Park, located in the southwestern province of Zeeland, unfolds as a testament to the dynamic interplay between tidal dynamics and marine life. This expansive estuary, part of the larger Delta Works project, showcases the resilience of coastal ecosystems and provides a vital habitat for seals, porpoises, and a diverse array of fish and invertebrates.

The Oosterscheldekering, a unique storm surge barrier that can be partially closed during extreme weather events, allows the tidal flow to continue, maintaining the estuary's ecological balance. Visitors can explore the park's coastline, encountering tidal flats, salt marshes, and iconic structures such as the Zeeland Bridge.

Oosterschelde National Park invites those with an appreciation for coastal dynamics and marine biodiversity to witness the ebb and flow of tides and the intricate dance of life within its waters. The park's commitment to sustainable management ensures that this estuarine landscape remains a thriving ecosystem that contributes to the ecological richness of the Dutch coastline.

Conclusion

The national parks of the Netherlands, with their diverse landscapes and ecosystems, stand as testament to the country's commitment to preserving and showcasing its natural heritage. From the ancient woodlands of Hoge Veluwe to the dynamic tidal dynamics of Oosterschelde, each park offers a unique window into the intricate relationship between nature and human stewardship.

These protected areas serve as havens for biodiversity, offering refuge to plant and animal species, and as sanctuaries for those seeking solace and connection with the natural world. The national parks of the Netherlands, woven into the fabric of the country's cultural and ecological tapestry, invite visitors to embark on a journey of exploration, appreciation, and conservation—a journey that celebrates the timeless beauty of nature in the heart of Europe.

Tulip Season - Blooms of Color

In the vibrant patchwork of the Dutch landscape, few spectacles rival the kaleidoscopic burst of color that heralds the arrival of tulip season. This annual phenomenon, marked by the breathtaking bloom of millions of tulips, transforms the lowlands into a living canvas of hues that captivate the imagination and draw visitors from around the globe. Tulip season in the Netherlands is not merely a floral display; it is a cultural celebration, an agricultural marvel, and a testament to the enduring allure of these iconic flowers.

A Tapestry of Colorful History

The story of tulips in the Netherlands is a tapestry woven with threads of history, trade, and horticultural innovation. While tulips are native to Central Asia, it was in the 16th century that they found their way to the Dutch Republic. Initially cultivated for their ornamental beauty, tulips soon became objects of fascination and desire, sparking a phenomenon known as "tulip mania."

During the Dutch Golden Age in the 17th century, tulip bulbs became coveted commodities, with prices soaring to extraordinary heights. The allure of these vibrant blooms captured the imaginations of artists, poets, and the Dutch elite. Today, tulips remain an integral part of the Dutch cultural landscape, symbolizing beauty, prosperity, and the arrival of spring.

The Keukenhof Gardens - A Floral Extravaganza

No exploration of tulip season in the Netherlands is complete without a visit to the Keukenhof Gardens, often referred to as the "Garden of Europe." Nestled in the heart of the Dutch flower-growing region in Lisse, Keukenhof is a horticultural marvel that spans over 32 hectares and showcases an astounding variety of tulips and other spring flowers.

The Keukenhof Gardens serve as a living canvas where landscaped gardens, thematic displays, and meticulously arranged flowerbeds create a visual symphony of color. Each year, the gardens welcome millions of visitors who come to witness the ephemeral beauty of tulip season. From early spring until late May, Keukenhof becomes a haven for flower enthusiasts, photographers, and those seeking inspiration from the boundless palette of nature.

The park's design, a collaboration of landscape architects, horticulturists, and artists, ensures a seamless integration of tulips with complementary flowers such as daffodils, hyacinths, and crocuses. The result is a sensory experience that goes beyond visual delight, as the fragrances of the flowers intermingle, creating an olfactory symphony that enhances the overall ambiance of the gardens.

The Tulip Fields - Endless Vistas of Color

Beyond the manicured landscapes of Keukenhof, the Dutch countryside transforms into a patchwork of tulip fields that stretch as far as the eye can see. The tulip fields, located primarily in the provinces of North Holland, South Holland, and Flevoland, offer a mesmerizing panorama of colors that evoke the spirit of spring.

As the tulips begin to bloom, typically from late March to early May, the fields become a canvas where farmers showcase their expertise in cultivating these delicate flowers. The carefully planned rows of tulips create an intricate mosaic, with each field featuring a distinct color palette and variety. From vibrant reds and pinks to serene whites and purples, the tulip fields embody the diversity of tulip species cultivated in the region.

Visitors can explore the tulip fields through various means, from guided tours and bicycle rides to hot air balloon excursions that provide an aerial perspective of the blooming landscapes. The experience of walking amidst the rows of tulips, feeling the soft petals against one's fingertips, and inhaling the sweet fragrance that permeates the air is an immersion into the very essence of tulip season in the Netherlands.

Cultivating Dutch Excellence - Tulip Farms and Growers

At the heart of tulip season are the dedicated tulip farms and growers who cultivate and nurture these iconic flowers with precision and passion. The Netherlands is globally renowned for its expertise in tulip cultivation, with Dutch tulip bulbs being sought after for their quality and variety.

Tulip farms, often family-owned and operated, play a pivotal role in the cultivation process. From carefully selecting and planting bulbs to monitoring growing conditions and implementing sustainable practices, tulip farmers employ a combination of tradition and innovation to ensure a bountiful bloom each spring. These farmers, who often have generations of experience, contribute to the legacy of Dutch tulip excellence.

In addition to tulip farms, the Netherlands is home to specialized bulb nurseries that focus on breeding and developing new tulip varieties. These nurseries collaborate with horticulturists and enthusiasts to introduce novel colors, shapes, and patterns to the world of tulips. The ongoing pursuit of excellence in tulip cultivation has made the Netherlands a global hub for bulb exports and a leader in the tulip industry.

Tulip Festivals - A Cultural Celebration

Tulip season in the Netherlands is not only an aesthetic delight but also a cultural celebration that manifests in various tulip festivals held across the country. These festivals, characterized by parades, exhibitions, and events, bring communities together to revel in the beauty of tulips and the arrival of spring.

One of the most renowned tulip festivals is the Bloemencorso Bollenstreek, or the Flower Parade of the Bulb Region. This spectacular event, held annually in April, features elaborately decorated floats adorned with tulips, hyacinths, and daffodils. The parade winds its way through the bulb-growing region, from Noordwijk to Haarlem, attracting thousands of spectators who gather to witness the floral procession.

In addition to parades, tulip festivals often include flower exhibitions, art installations, and cultural performances. These events not only showcase the aesthetic diversity of tulips but also celebrate their cultural significance in Dutch history and heritage.

Tulip Culture and Symbolism - Beyond Beauty

The tulip, with its graceful form and vibrant colors, has transcended its role as a decorative flower to become a symbol deeply ingrained in Dutch culture. Beyond its aesthetic appeal, the tulip holds cultural and historical significance, embodying themes of wealth, love, and the ephemeral nature of beauty.

The tulip's association with the Dutch Golden Age and the tulip mania of the 17th century has left an indelible mark on the country's cultural narrative. The flower's symbolic value extends to various aspects of Dutch life, from art and literature to national events and festivities. Today, the tulip is not just a flower; it is a cultural icon that continues to inspire and unite.

In the language of flowers, tulips carry diverse meanings. Red tulips symbolize love and passion, yellow tulips represent cheerful thoughts, and white tulips convey forgiveness and purity. The range of hues and varieties allows individuals to express sentiments and emotions through the gift of tulips, making them a cherished part of various celebrations and occasions.

Sustainable Tulip Farming - Balancing Beauty and Responsibility

As tulip season attracts increasing numbers of visitors each year, there is a growing awareness of the need for sustainable practices in tulip farming. Balancing the beauty of tulip cultivation with environmental responsibility has become a priority for farmers and the Dutch horticultural industry as a whole.

Sustainable tulip farming involves practices such as responsible water management, soil conservation, and the use of environmentally friendly pesticides. Many tulip farms are adopting organic farming methods to minimize their ecological footprint and preserve the natural balance of the landscapes where tulips bloom.

Furthermore, initiatives such as bulb recycling programs aim to reduce waste and promote the reuse of tulip bulbs. By addressing environmental concerns and embracing sustainable practices, the Dutch tulip industry is ensuring that future generations can continue to enjoy the mesmerizing beauty of tulip season without compromising the health of the ecosystems that support it.

Photographing Tulip Season - Capturing Nature's Palette

For photographers, tulip season in the Netherlands presents a unique and captivating subject that demands both skill and artistry. The challenge lies not only in capturing the vivid colors and intricate details of tulips but also in conveying the essence of the season—the spirit of renewal and the fleeting beauty of nature's cycles.

Photographers flock to tulip fields and gardens armed with cameras, lenses, and an eye for composition. The changing light throughout the day, from the soft hues of sunrise to the golden glow of sunset, adds a dynamic dimension to the photographic opportunities. The juxtaposition of tulips with other spring flowers, windmills, and traditional Dutch landscapes enhances the storytelling potential of each frame.

Capturing the essence of tulip season goes beyond technical proficiency; it requires an appreciation for the interplay of colors, textures, and light. Photographers often seek unique perspectives, experimenting with angles and compositions to convey the immersive experience of being surrounded by a sea of tulips.

Tulip Season Beyond Blooms - Year-Round Appreciation

While tulip season in the Netherlands is a concentrated burst of color during the spring months, the appreciation for tulips extends throughout the year. The Dutch tulip industry operates year-round, encompassing bulb cultivation, breeding programs, and international exports.

Tulip bulbs, the unsung heroes of the blooming season, undergo a meticulous process of cultivation, harvesting, and storage. Expertise in bulb handling ensures the quality and vitality of tulips, allowing for their distribution to markets worldwide. The tulip bulb trade is not only a vital component of the horticultural industry but also contributes to the global popularity of tulips as ornamental flowers.

Beyond the Netherlands, tulips have become a global symbol of beauty and resilience. Various countries cultivate and celebrate tulips, incorporating them into their landscapes, festivals, and cultural practices. The international appeal of tulips transcends borders, making them a shared source of inspiration and joy.

Conclusion

Tulip season in the Netherlands is more than a visual spectacle; it is a celebration of nature's artistry, cultural heritage, and the enduring connection between people and flowers. From the meticulously landscaped gardens of Keukenhof to the sprawling tulip fields that stretch across the Dutch countryside, tulip season invites visitors into a world of color, fragrance, and the timeless beauty of spring.

As tulips unfurl their petals in a riot of hues, they carry with them the rich history of Dutch horticulture, the cultural symbolism of the flower, and a reminder of the delicate balance between nature's bounty and responsible stewardship. Tulip season is a testament to the enduring allure of these iconic flowers and the profound impact they have had on the cultural identity of the Netherlands—a country where each bloom is not just a flower but a brushstroke in the masterpiece of tulip season.

Epilogue: A Farewell to the Netherlands

As your journey through the Netherlands comes to a close, we bid you farewell with a heart full of memories and a mind enriched by the diverse tapestry of Dutch experiences. From the bustling streets of Amsterdam to the serene landscapes of national parks, you've traversed a country that seamlessly blends history, culture, and nature.

Reflect on the iconic windmills that stand as sentinels of a bygone era and the modern marvels of Rotterdam that signify the Netherlands' commitment to progress. Remember the tulip fields, ablaze with color during the ephemeral beauty of spring, and the tranquil canals that weave through centuries-old cities.

The Netherlands, with its rich heritage and warm hospitality, has left an indelible mark on your journey. As you carry these memories with you, remember that the essence of the Dutch spirit lies not only in the landmarks you've visited but in the connections you've made—with the people, the landscapes, and the stories that unfolded at every turn.

May the tulips you witnessed in full bloom serve as a reminder of the fleeting yet profound beauty of life. As you embark on new adventures, may the lessons learned from the Dutch commitment to sustainability and cultural preservation inspire a similar stewardship in your own explorations.

Whether this guide has been your companion on a physical journey or a vicarious exploration from the comfort of your armchair, we hope it has ignited a passion for discovery and a deeper appreciation for the wonders that the Netherlands has to offer.

As you step away from the pages of "Discovering the Netherlands: A Comprehensive Travel Guide," know that the spirit of this enchanting country accompanies you. Until we meet again on the shores of the IJsselmeer or amidst the tulip fields in bloom, may your travels be filled with curiosity, joy, and the enduring magic of exploration.

Safe travels and tot ziens!

Appendix: Additional Resources

For travelers seeking more in-depth information, planning tips, and further exploration of the Netherlands, this appendix provides a curated list of additional resources. From official tourism boards to recommended reading materials, these sources aim to enhance your understanding and experience of the diverse facets of Dutch culture, history, and attractions.

Official Tourism Resources:

1. **Netherlands Board of Tourism & Conventions (NBTC):**
   - Website: Visit Holland[1]
   - Explore the official tourism website for the Netherlands, offering comprehensive information on destinations, activities, and travel essentials.

2. **City Tourism Websites:**
   - I amsterdam[2] (Amsterdam)
   - Rotterdam Tourist Information[3] (Rotterdam)
   - The Hague Marketing[4] (The Hague)
   - Visit Utrecht[5] (Utrecht)
   - Haarlem Marketing[6] (Haarlem)
   - Delft Marketing[7] (Delft)
   - Maastricht Marketing[8] (Maastricht)

Travel Guides:

1. https://www.holland.com/

2. https://www.iamsterdam.com/

3. https://en.rotterdam.info/

4. https://denhaag.com/en

5. https://www.visit-utrecht.com/

6. https://www.visithaarlem.com/en/

7. https://www.delft.com/

8. https://www.visitmaastricht.com/

1. **Lonely Planet - Netherlands:**
   - Author: Lonely Planet
   - A comprehensive travel guide covering various aspects of Dutch travel, from cultural attractions to practical travel tips.
2. **Rick Steves' Amsterdam & the Netherlands:**
   - Author: Rick Steves
   - Renowned travel expert Rick Steves provides insights into exploring Amsterdam and other Dutch destinations, offering practical advice and cultural context.
3. **Rough Guide to the Netherlands:**
   - Authors: Rough Guides
   - A detailed guidebook offering a deeper understanding of the Netherlands, including historical context, local insights, and off-the-beaten-path recommendations.

Cultural and Historical Reading:

1. **"The Dutch Republic: Its Rise, Greatness, and Fall 1477–1806" by Jonathan Israel:**
   - A comprehensive historical account of the rise and fall of the Dutch Republic, providing insights into the political, economic, and cultural developments.
2. **"The Diary of Anne Frank" by Anne Frank:**
   - A poignant firsthand account of Jewish life during World War II, as documented by Anne Frank in her diary while hiding from the Nazis in Amsterdam.
3. **"The Hiding Place" by Corrie ten Boom:**
   - The memoir of Corrie ten Boom, a Dutch Christian who, along with her family, helped Jews escape the Nazis during the Holocaust.

Art and Culture:

1. **"The Rijksmuseum: Deluxe Edition" by Wim Pijbes:**
   - A visually stunning book showcasing the highlights of Amsterdam's Rijksmuseum, including masterpieces by Dutch artists such as Rembrandt and Vermeer.
2. **"Girl with a Pearl Earring" by Tracy Chevalier:**
   - While a work of fiction, this novel is inspired by Vermeer's famous painting and offers a fictionalized glimpse into the artist's life and the cultural milieu of 17th-century Delft.

Nature and Parks:

1. **"Walking in the Ardennes: Wallonia, Belgium and Luxembourg" by Jeff Williams:**
   - While focused on the Ardennes region, this guidebook includes information on hiking trails that extend into the southern part of the Netherlands.
2. **"Wild Flowers of the Mediterranean: A Complete Guide to the Islands and Coastal Regions" by Marjorie Blamey and Christopher Grey-Wilson:**
   - A useful resource for those interested in the diverse flora, including wildflowers, found in the Mediterranean climate of parts of the Netherlands.

Tulip Season:

1. **"Tulipomania: The Story of the World's Most Coveted Flower & the Extraordinary Passions It Aroused" by Mike Dash:**
   - An engaging historical account of the tulip mania that swept through 17th-century Netherlands, providing

context for the enduring fascination with tulips.

2. **"The Flower Yard: Growing Flamboyant Flowers in Containers" by Arthur Parkinson:**
   - While not specific to the Netherlands, this book offers practical insights into growing vibrant flowers, including tulips, in containers.

Language Resources:

1. **Duolingo - Dutch:**
   - Website: Duolingo Dutch[9]
   - A language-learning platform offering Dutch courses for beginners, providing a basic understanding of the language.
2. **"Dutch for Dummies" by Margreet Kwakernaak:**
   - A practical guide for learning Dutch, suitable for beginners and those looking to improve their language skills.

Online Platforms:

1. **Reddit - r/Netherlands:**
   - r/Netherlands[10]
   - An online community where travelers and locals share experiences, advice, and insights about the Netherlands.
2. **Instagram - #Netherlands:**
   - Instagram Netherlands[11]
   - Explore the visual beauty of the Netherlands through the lens of Instagram, where users share captivating

9. https://www.duolingo.com/

10. https://www.reddit.com/r/thenetherlands/

11. https://www.instagram.com/explore/tags/netherlands/

images of Dutch landscapes, architecture, and culture.

These resources aim to provide a well-rounded and enriched experience for those exploring the Netherlands. Whether you're interested in historical narratives, practical travel tips, or cultural insights, the curated selection caters to a range of interests and preferences. Happy exploring!

Printed by Libri Plureos GmbH in Hamburg,
Germany